Fires

Hardship, Grief and Perseverance

A collection of poetry by
ULLIE-KAYE

fires.

and if you have ever been abandoned.
be a constant. if you have ever been
wrapped up in nights so dark, you
could not find your way back home.
be light. if you have ever fallen
apart into a thousand, fractured
pieces and wondered where on earth
everyone has gone. be present. if you
have ever felt unworthy. unbeautiful.
unseen. unknown. unheard. be love.
i tell you the truth. some of the most
precious things we learn, are from
the fires that we've endured.

ullie-kaye

repression.

stop trying to be so strong.
do you know what happens when
you keep holding it all together?
you eventually fall apart anyways.
whether it is through anger.
or addiction. or self injury.
or illness. repression will kill you.
fall apart now while it's still
fresh and begging to be released.
whoever said you were weak for
hurting out loud, has some falling
apart of their own to do.

ullie-kaye

delicate.

sometimes when i feel delicate, i find
warmth in things that feel like the
kind of fire that will not burn out.
i tell myself about all of the times
that i did something brave and i hold
them up to the light and remember my
strength. sometimes when i feel delicate,
i take a minute to step outside. to meet
with the morning. to bask my skin in sun
for awhile. and i smile. i take a deep
breath and inhale the goodness that is
surrounding me. and i stay there for as
long as it takes to know that i am not
alone. sometimes when i feel delicate,
i look at my hands and try to see what
makes them full. and what makes them
empty. and how will i keep them from
trembling so. and then i raise them up
towards the skies in honor of my journey.
even if they are weak. and tired. even if
they still do not fully believe in the
power of miracles. and fighting. and the
newness of day. and i dance with my shadow
to a song i don't know. and i grow.

ullie-kaye

boats.

different storms.
different boats.
different oceans altogether.
but yet the same, deep longing
for healing. you do not need
to minimize what you are
going through. you do not
need to measure. suppress.
or compare. you can still
find perspective in it all.
dear human, regardless of
its shape. intensity. or variety.
your pain is always valid.

ullie-kaye

one day.

one day, if you haven't already, you will
wish you had slowed down. taken time for
the small things. saved an injured bird.
watched the sky more closely. learned the
names of clouds. memorized the lyrics.
the poem. the lines on somebody's face.
one day, if you haven't already, you will
wish you had talked to the soul on the
corner. cardboard sign waving. but still
with a story. asking for money but needing
a friend. one day, if you haven't already,
you will wish you had taken the vacation.
the sick leave. the offer for help. because
you will be tired. and worn. and aching
in places that keep you from gathering
yourself up the way that you used to.
your spirit will dance but your body will
settle for watching the others. one day,
if you haven't already, you will not carry
grudges. you will not speak without thinking.
you will not worry about whether or not you
are beautiful. because you will already know.
you are.

　　　　ullie-kaye

journey.

i love the kind of people who are
on a raw and beautiful journey
towards self. they are at a place
in life where they have come to
understand that you can have
everything you ever thought you
needed and still end up feeling
empty. they have learned that the
world does not even remotely revolve
around material things but rather
all of the fires they have had to
walk through. and learn from. and
make peace with. they do not hide
their flaws because they know that
there is no shame in imperfection.
they recognize that the process of
healing and growing and becoming,
is ongoing. they will forever be a
work in progress.

ullie-kaye

brave thing.

it has not been easy for you. to choose
with intention. to make kindness a way
of life. to defend those who have not
always shown you love. to speak up when
the silences became too deafening. to have
faith in something so big that it rumbled
inside of your chest. to listen to those
who thought and believed and breathed
differently than you did. to admit your
faults. and say sorry. to wear your heart
just a little bit closer to your sleeve.
to make a promise to yourself - and keep it.
to face the monsters. the grief. the trauma.
to heal. to let go when it wasn't yours to
carry. and to hold on when everything
seemed to be falling apart. to find laughter
even when it did not roll like water off
your tongue. to embrace the path. to dream.
to cry. now go. make something beautiful.
you are a brave thing, after all.

ullie-kaye

weightless.

as a sensitive soul, you need time to recharge.
you carry everything so deeply and personally
that it feels nearly impossible to separate your
pain from that of others. and so, you find
yourself in a constant state of overwhelm.
not because you do not want to love so hard but
because you love so hard and do not remember
how to replenish all of the emotional work that
you have done. and perhaps you can never become
truly weightless. but you can begin here.
subdue the fires. return to nature. worship.
meet with like-minded hearts. soak your eyes
in old photographs. drink up peace. dance to
silence. light a candle. marinate yourself in
scripture. poetry. music. art. prayer. inhale
the breath of quiet contemplation. run with all
your might towards tranquility. find comfort
in your own presence. just you. your thoughts.
and the maker of the universe. you are worth
every ounce of this. believe me. your body will
thank you.

ullie-kaye

wounds.

you are not your wounds, dear one.
they cling to your skin like a
battle you cannot depart from.
they emerge at every crossroads.
every heartbreak. every starless
night. and every sunless morning.
they remind you that they are
still sometimes raw and vulnerable
and at the brink of splitting wide
open again. but you are not your
wounds, dear one. you are light.
and courage. and wisdom. you are
soft and tender words. and growth
that may otherwise never have had
a chance. you are an anchor,
holding fast. you are drenched
with overcoming. you are beautiful
in ways that only those who have
felt war, could ever understand.
and when i look at the grace with
which you love the others. how you
water their gardens. how you shine
on their sadness. i see it.
the wonder in you is there because
of the wounds in you.

ullie-kaye

9

learning.

i have devoted myself to learning. it is,
after all, in the hallways of my mind,
where i tend to all of the beauty and the
mess. and in these days where i have lived
long enough to know that life can be both
cruel and kind. that it takes just a moment
for everything to change. that the things
we once believed meant something, may not
need to take up so much space. and by the
same token, those things we lost along the
way; the loves we knew. the tenderness with
which we saw the world. the simple graces
that used to take our breath away. oh how
we miss them now. the passage of time has
done something to me. and in my willingness
to listen, i have gained a piece of wisdom.
perhaps darkness is only light that has yet
to be endured.

ullie-kaye

alive.

i do not have a fear of dying. i fear living
without having loved with my arms wider
than an open field. without having put on
all of my armor for the battle and giving up
before it was finished. i fear that i will not
use my gifts to my very last breath. that i
will grow quiet. or tired. or too jaded to see
art in every human being. to lose my gasp
at every bleeding sky. i fear living without
having carried out a promise. without having
said "i'm sorry". or made peace with every
creature that has ever crossed my path.
without having told myself at least once a
day that i was beautiful - and meant it from
the pit of my ribcage. that i did not wake up
every morning and reach for something simply
because i was told it was impossible. i do not
have a fear of dying. i have a fear of living,
without being fully alive.

ullie-kaye

what love does.

i want you to know that i would drink
the ocean dry of its fury if it meant
that your storm would rage a little less
wildly. and i would graft the marrow of
my own bones into your weariness if it
meant that you felt a little bit stronger.
like a tree growing upwards and outwards
and into the sky. i would carry you a
thousand miles and then a thousand miles
more if it meant that you could start fresh.
feel renewed. be further along the path.
heal your wounds. taste a sliver of hope
again. and i guess what i am really trying
to say is that i am not doing this because
i have to. not even for a moment. i am doing
this because i want to. that's just what
love does.

ullie-kaye

gracious.

be gracious. some of us are still
bruised from yesterday's battles.
some of us are hurting but healing.
some of us are finding the shapes
and patterns of where we fit in
and we are running out of places
that feel like home. we are wearing
thin on empty promises. we are tired.
and fragile. and fumbling. and sometimes
we are not at our best and it shows.
so be gracious. i promise, we're trying.
and we will be gracious, too.

ullie-kaye

walls.

i don't want to play it safe anymore.
i don't want to build these walls, like
mountains, shielding me. i don't want
to run from the past or hide from the
future. i don't want to live like i'm
dying or die while i'm living. i don't
want to fall apart without falling
together. or hurt without learning.
or have without giving. i don't want to
take these stars for granted. these lights
that burn incessantly upon my face even
while i'm sleeping. they do not give up
on me with their steady glow. not once
have they left my side. let me collide
with possibility. and second chances.
and the kind of hope that is palpable.
let me wear the skin of a soul salvaged
by grace. a holy place. a warm embrace.
and nothing more.

ullie-kaye

wander.

and if nothing else.
if these wounds do not heal.
if i crumble underneath the
weight. if i lose the ones i
love along the way. if i forget
how to gather up courage like
flowers from a river bed and
fill my lungs with breath.
i will keep my heart soft.
i will keep my lantern burning.
i will not compromise who
i am. and i will leave this
earth a fragrant place for
those who have yet to wander
within it.

ullie-kaye

rock bottom.

rock bottom will rattle your
bones. make no mistake of it.
you will know when you have
arrived. but you will not unpack
your bags. you will not lower
the lights. and you will not
turn down the covers and crawl
into bed. because you are not
staying, my love. you are not
staying.

ullie-kaye

feel.

so feel then. feel. whatever it is
that is lingering deep and begging
to come to the surface. whether grief.
or anger. or sadness. or trepidation.
too many of us bury things for fear
they might hurt when they emerge.
they will. so feel them first. their
soft curves or their jagged edges.
invite them in. honor and apoint their
place and purpose in your life.
then decide whether or not they have
reason to stay.

   ullie-kaye

something bigger.

my heart tells me that i am not
immune to breaking. nature tells
me that i am one, small star within
ten billion galaxies. reason tells
me that i am just a mortal, fighting
against an inevitable end. pain tells
me that life is hard; to live and love
one breath at a time. and faith tells
me that i need to believe in something
much bigger than myself.

ullie-kaye

missing piece.

if i have learned anything at
all in these years of traveling
the sun, it is this. people are
searching. they are reaching.
and yearning. they are burning
the candle at both ends. going
through the motions. falling
through the cracks. wanting to
connect somehow but feeling so
inept in a world that keeps
redefining what connection means.
and how it's done. and does it even
feel like love anymore?
there are broken ones among us.
they are everywhere. hiding
amongst sweet smiles and wide
skylines. glimmering as though
they are fulfilled. while inside
they ache. they long for something
more. a missing piece, perhaps.
or maybe just missing - peace.

                    ullie-kaye

olive branch.

over and over again, you chose
to give and love and create
space for peace. not only that,
but you extended it outward
like an olive branch. a calm
in the storm. a quiet place.
a lighthouse in the darkness.
even when you had every right
to feel bitter. and to sink
low. and to take your heart
off of your sleeve and let it
grow cold. even when you had
inner work of your own to do.
and i just wanted you to know
that i think your strength is
really beautiful.

ullie-kaye

wildfire.

i am inclined to believe that we have all made
mistakes. that we have all gone through seasons
of darkness. that we have all, at one time or
another, experienced some form of loss and have
carried grief on our shoulders like clouds that
just would not soften. i am inclined to believe
that we have all danced around words that should
have been said. and unleashed the ones that should
never have turned into daggers and gone after
their hearts. and i am inclined to believe that
we have all felt the sting of loneliness. of sadness.
of hurt. and feeling like we do not belong. we have
quietly wished for more out of life. let ourselves
fall by the wayside. settled for artificial light
when all along we had access to the stars. but we
looked the other way. we looked the other way.
there are two things i know that spread like
wildfire. love and fear. and we chose fear sometimes.
may we know now, how great an honor it is to be
engulfed by flames. and to walk out a different
person on the other side.

ullie-kaye

21

heartbeat.

if we can self destruct then
we can heal. if we can fall,
defeated then we can rise in
power. if we can grow weary
then we can grow mighty.
if we can be drenched in light
and still feel the darkness
then we can be drenched in
darkness and still feel the
light. what i am trying to say,
good soul, is that i can still
hear your heartbeat. and where
there is a heartbeat, there is
a way back home.

ullie-kaye

healers.

it takes a wounded soul to fully understand
another wounded soul, i am convinced of it.
some of the most precious humans that i have
come to know are caregivers because they too,
have been there once. where it was dark.
or burdensome. or eerily quiet. they have had
to fight for something. struggle through.
come face to face with decisions that no one
should ever have to make. and now look at how
they bravely shine their light for everybody
else to see. tending to the broken. mending.
always mending. still with a few missing pieces
here and there but loving brightly nonetheless.
what a beautiful thing it is to give because you
have known lacking and longing and loneliness.
i have come to believe that the hurt ones are
also the healers.

ullie-kaye

survive.

i wish i could have told her that she
would see many beautiful days.
sunrises and sunsets that would nearly
take her breath away. that she would
warm herself by the fire and feel like
all is well with the world. that no one
could ever steal her joy or enthusiasm
or the dreams on her taste buds. but i
wish too, that i could have told her that
she would see starless nights. empty hands.
mountains of grief. eyes, once filled with
light and wonder, turning to grey.
that she would question her own strength.
her faith. her purpose. and her journey.
and that somehow she would survive it all.

ullie-kaye

faith.

faith does not begin where fear ends.
she comes when you are still lying in
the bottom of the gutter. hands trembling.
doubts running rampant. seas stormy.
breath insufficient. darkness winning.
thoughts blurring. skies fading. more black
than blue. obstructed view. no way through.
there. in the absence. in the tragedy.
in the emptiness. in the wreckage that made
its way into the very marrow of your bones.
in the fire that could not be drenched.
in the thirst that could not be quenched.
in the wounds that would not heal. in the
heart that could not feel. in the broken.
the lost. and surreal. that's when she comes.

ullie-kaye

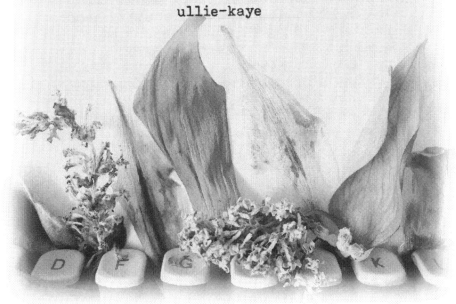

25

no bashful thing.

love is no bashful thing. it burrows through
deep places. to mend. and hold. and believes
in something much bigger. and better. it lays
beside grief and brings a lantern. it does
not hurry your healing. your journey. your
path towards peace. love is no bashful thing.
it listens to your heartbeat. your heartbreak.
your heartsong. and finds the rhythm of your
soul. and in those tragic moments where breath
becomes dark and scarce and unforgiving. love
throws no stones. but rather aims to understand.
love is no bashful thing. it travels uphill, both
ways. barefoot. and bleeding. and beautifully
brave. it lessens the load. it builds a boat.
it faces the wind and walks through the waves.
love is no bashful thing.

ullie-kaye

26

here.

some things will always be completely
out of our hands. it is one of the most
helpless and hopeless feelings to experience.
to know that we cannot make it better.
we cannot change it. control it. or wave
our magic wand and make it go away.
it just isn't within our grasp, nor was
it meant to be. but yet we try, don't we?
to make ourselves god. to hang the stars
and orchestrate their shimmer. because
the unknown is such a wretched place.
but here, where we cannot touch the things
that glide in and out of our existence
is where we must learn to find peace.
precisely here. in the midst of the timing
we did not ask for. in the circumstances
we did not approve of. and in the storm
that even with all our strength, we could
not bring ourselves to silence.

ullie-kaye

time.

i am not always strong.
i am not always brave.
and i have not even remotely
come to a place where i can
look back and say that i
have finally made it through.
because there are lessons
that need to be relearned
every morning. like waiting.
and inhaling peace. and
showing myself the same
grace as i would anybody else.
some of the most precious
things in life, take time.

                ullie-kaye

a time.

i am a giver. i am open hands.
full. spilling over. nurturer.
listener. strong soldier. let me
hold you. go the distance. friend.
but i can tell you beyond the
shadow of a doubt that were it not
for the ocean of times that i was
on the receiving end, that i would
not have learned humility and
compassion and grace and the
importance of raw, human emotion.
i would not have learned how
beautiful it is to feel safe enough
to cry. to speak. to bleed. to seep.
and let myself be held. i would not
have learned the art of needing to
be loved in ways that are far from
being easy. or ordinary. or elegant.
or glorious. so just be there.
whichever way your heart is leaning.
sometimes blessing.
sometimes blessed.
there is a time.

                ullie-kaye

29

river.

i am not the best at holding back.
you see, i am a river, flowing wild.
bursting at the seams. if i love you,
you will know because i cannot hide
it. i am heavy rains on windowpanes.
deep embers. star-filled nights.
i can not show you just the half
of me for the other half will only
blow in with the wind. the tides.
the ships at sea. a storm waiting
eagerly to tell you everything.
my deepest secrets. and my most
fragrant dreams. i am door wide
open. heart hurt but healing.
and the more i've lost the more i
choose to risk it all. to live.
to love. to leave a legacy.
i will defend your brokenness because
i have been there too. but i will not
hold back. it's just not in me to do.

ullie-kaye

the way.

sometimes the weak carry
the weak. not because they
have the strength but simply
because they know the way.

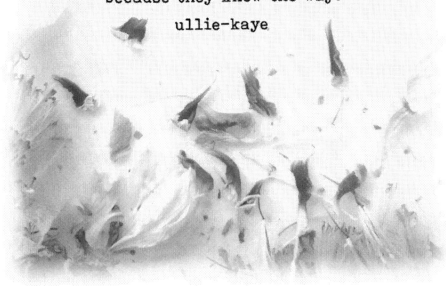 ullie-kaye

misunderstood.

i am both an empath and an intellect.
full of wild and full of peace.
fractured in too many places to count
and as whole as whole can be.
sometimes i am a giver while at the same
time, in desperate need of receiving.
i can be surrounded yet lonely.
or alone yet blissfully fulfilled.
i am quietly brave. and loudly different.
i laugh when i'm nervous and cry
at the drop of a hat. sometimes i run
towards the same troubled waters
as i try to save others from.
i am often misunderstood. but that's okay.
i am still learning to understand myself
too.

ullie-kaye

reprieve.

some days i feel like i am falling
apart. and some days i feel like
i am finally falling together.
and in some, strange way, i have
found this to be the sweet elixir
of life. to love myself in the calm
and in the storm. and to believe
with all my heart that i am meant
to inhale both kinds of weather.
that if it were not for the chaos,
i would not cherish the reprieve.

ullie-kaye

close.

how precious is life that it can be so full of
exuberance one day and so full of clinging
to our own breath the next. from fierce to
fragile. from glory to grim. we cannot predict
what this earth has in store for us. and we
cannot measure the infinite possibilities of
why things must sometimes go the way that
they do. but let us at the very least, recognize
this truth. that we are not immortal. not one
of us. we are not immune to pain. and change.
and loss. and storms that wreak havoc on our
most sacred places. even when all is well and
good and overflowing. we are always at the mercy
of one, single blunder. one mishap. one wrong turn.
this, my souls, is why we must not take any of it
all for granted. the beauty and the tragedy.
hold each other close.

ullie-kaye

light chasers.

and while they are chasing after things that
do not fill them, we will chase after the light.
that is not to say that we will not, once in a
tender while, stumble over particles of darkness.
pain is inevitable. but we will search evermore
for that which the empty spaces of this world
cannot give us. we will seek after bright souls.
and if they are not bright, we will leave them
always knowing how much they are loved. we will
hunt for grace. and if we cannot find it, we will
soak our eyes in the storms that could have taken
us but in mercy, washed us instead. we will look
for the gardens. and if we cannot find them,
we will bury our breaths in the sweet scent of
forgiveness. we will leave no stone unturned.
and sometimes we will lose our way.
but that's okay.
even the stars fall from time to time.

ullie-kaye

make light.

we will cry together, okay?
we will bring our crumpled spirits
and weave joy out of whatever it is
that we can find. we will dance to
sad songs and search for stars among
the blackest of skies. we will make
the hard things softer. and lean on
one another's shoulders. we will learn
about scars and suffering and new
ways to make light. we will trust.
and love. and worship through it all.
we will stay sturdy. our hearts will
be anchors. and shelters. and shores.
we will look up and be still and
gather our courage. we will defy
everything that we were told we could
not do. and we will not abandon ship.
we were made for this.

ullie-kaye

wings.

i hope that you find what you are
looking for. but i hope that what you
are looking for is driven only by
things like love. and mending. and a
soul at peace with where it resides.
i hope that all of the parts of you
that still remain fragile, grow sturdier
and braver with time. that you choose
sometimes, to do the harder things in
life so that when you encounter an
unexpected storm, you will already
have some flight behind your wings.
i hope you feel deeply. and fall with
arms wide open beneath you. i hope
you heal. even if you do not yet know
where the path is leading you. i hope
you find your spirit in tact and filling.
that you find the kind of water that
quenches your thirst and the kind of
shelter that does not crumble. i hope
that you are able to find something
beautiful in the ordinary and something
to hold on to when the winds change
direction. and i hope that somewhere
along the way, you find yourself too.

ullie-kaye

jewels.

feast your soul on the beautiful truth.
you are here in this precise fraction of
time because you were made for it.
whatever that means for you. you have
oceans colliding inside of your chest -
i know. sometimes they rage and sometimes,
they flow. and i cannot begin to fathom
all the things that swim through your
veins. the days you were drunk on life and
the days you were sobered by grief so thick,
it clung to your lips like expired milk. listen.
your heart is begging you. look for the jewels.
whether in the sun as she glistens through
your window. or in an old, record shop, filled
from floor to sky with music that brings you
back. hold your head high at knowing that
you never once gave up on love, even at the
risk of losing it all. that in the quiet of
your own spirit, you did everything you could
to find your way. even when you did so alone.
but then again, you were never really alone,
you were just being held. and you were never
really lost, you were just without a path.
and even with all that you have carried, you
refused to stop believing in one more day.
and one more day again. soak yourself in this.
heartbreak is loud. but darling, healing
is louder.
                    ullie-kaye

38

breaths.

and so we carry on our breaths
here on earth. full of ache.
and emptiness. full of love and
risk and euphoria. full of days
that feel like years and years
that fly like the blink of an
eye. and it's all right there.
all of it. in lingering pangs.
or in flashes of time. sad goodbyes.
and blissful mornings. coffee.
and music. and conversations.
seas that dance wildly and seas
that lay so still, we can almost
hear our own thoughts suspended
in the air. and i cannot help but
wonder at how brave it is that we
were made with the capacity to
hold so much at once.

ullie-kaye

falling.

if we only knew then what we know now.
that love conquers everything. that faith
can move mountains. that good things
happen to bad people and bad things
happen to good people. that loud doesn't
mean strong and quiet doesn't mean weak.
that closed hearts are often hurt hearts
that have yet to unfold. that silence can be
both beautiful and terrifying. that healing
takes time and time moves both quickly
and unbearably slowly. that one step in
any direction can change the course of
your life forever. that bliss is sometimes
just loving what you already have rather
than wanting what you wish you had. that
you will have days where you feel on top of
the world and days where you feel like you
have hit rock bottom. and that rising from
the ashes requires going through the flames.
and that falling was part of it all.

ullie-kaye

planted.

you cannot draw water from an
empty well. neither can you pour
from it. emptiness produces emptiness.
you cannot ask the storm for permission.
you take the storm and you drench
it with every ounce of fire inside
of you – and then some. you cannot
expect light to follow you home.
you hunt for it. you dig. and gather.
and climb treacherous mountains.
you cannot love without vulnerability.
without accepting that to love fully
means to risk loss. and to risk loss,
is to allow your soul to crack open
in every direction, both deep and wide,
even if it ends in goodbye. you cannot
learn without listening. or rise without
falling. you cannot grow without being
planted. and if you are to be planted,
you must endure the darkness.
it is the only way.

ullie-kaye

comfort zones.

in your heart of hearts you
already know. do not question
the still, small voice that is
telling you which way to go.
you are afraid because things
will be different. feel different.
but then again, you are braver
now than you were back then.
and you have learned that strength
does not grow from comfort zones.
it grows from thorns. and high tides.
and wild, wild winds that knock
you off of your feet.

ullie-kaye

home.

some need to be carried softly.
for they have just been through
storm-filled waters with jagged
edges. some need to be told they
are loved. for they have just spent
a lifetime waiting for those words
like jewels, dripping from mouths
that really mean it for once.
some need a place to weep the tears
they have collected in bottles for
years of safekeeping. some need a
voice of reason. for every lens
they have looked through has been
tainted and blurred by hurt. and
fear. and insecurity. and mistrust.
and some just need a place to call
home. to set down their bags and
hang their photographs and look
through the kitchen window at the
backyard and finally know that
not everything in life will be
transient. that some were meant to
stay. and that love will always
find a way.

                    ullie-kaye

43

flicker.

sometimes the ones who emanate
the brightest light also absorb
the greatest darkness. and somehow
even while carrying their own
burdens, they nurture others.
they hold out their hands. they
breathe their courage into the
lungs of those who are quietly
fading. all they know is how to
give. and that life feels better
when they burn. when they build a
roaring fire for the empty hearted.
the lonely. the ones without a path.
but the truth is, our bodies know.
and if not yet, they will. you cannot
fully live off of a flicker.

ullie-kaye

promise me.

stay in the light, okay?
no matter what it takes.
promise me.
troubles will come.
there is no question.
waves will overwhelm.
your heart will break.
your soul will quake.
and you will lose your way.
but only for a moment.
only for a moment.

ullie-kaye

hold on.

promise me this.
if they all abandon you.
if you are left wandering aimlessly.
if the hurt in your heart takes up
more space than the hope in your heart.
if you have lost everything that you
believed meant something to you.
if you are emptier now than the sound
of your own echo - you hold on.
you stay by your side.
you look to the skies.
you remember your whys.
and you do not abandon yourself.

ullie-kaye

tender.

it is okay to feel things heavily
for awhile. you are, after all,
still tender in so many places.
and healing takes time. it takes
work. and perseverance. there
will be peaks and there will be
valleys. there will be glimpses
of hope and unanswered questions.
but we can know this with all
certainty. we are not alone.
we are not forgotten. and we will
somehow find the strength we need.
this journey was not meant for
the faint of heart.

ullie-kaye

change.

if you have encountered too many
wolves in life, become a shepherd.
if you have encountered too much
loss in life, become a guide. if you
have encountered too much pain in
life, become a healer. if you have
encountered too much hatred in life,
embody compassion. may we always
aim to be the very things that our
hearts and souls seek. hurricanes
to hillsides. wilderness to waters.
fires into fragrant fields. this is
where we find comfort; knowing that
inside us all, is the capacity to love.
and where love resides, there is the
courage to change.

ullie-kaye

this grief.

and for the first time, i do not
know what it is that i am holding
onto. were it anger, i would not
feel like these tears could fill up
every sea with their salt-stained
emotion. were it sadness, i would
not feel like i was overflowing with
the rage of a thousand wild and
uncaged horses. were it fear, i would
not feel like i could make the earth
tremble by the strength of my own,
sheer willpower to keep on fighting.
so what is it then, this grief?
so enormous that it can only be
defined by both the absolute absence
and the absolute presence of love
itself.

ullie-kaye

bare bones.

hope is not always soft and lovely.
she is not always cascading rivers
and sunlit skies, dancing. hope knows
there is work to be done. there are
roads to be traveled. turns to be made.
she is bare bones and deep waters.
she is weary and weak. she is barely
a glimmer. she shakes when she speaks.
this is where hope lives. smothered in
sweat. full of war. and on the verge
of crumbling into the sea.
yet there she is, quietly breathing.

ullie-kaye

i miss us.

i miss us.
i miss we. and let's.
and together.
i miss laughing.
and crying.
and finishing each
            each other's sentences.

ullie-kaye

these human hearts.

these human hearts, they hold
so much. oceans full of chaos.
mountains of grief. hurricanes
that come without sirens and turn
everything we ever knew upon its
head. and perhaps we are all just
weary souls, playing hide and seek
with our demons. running for
shelter but knowing full well that
one day we will have to look the
storm dead in the eye and say,
"enough. enough of this".
so all that is left then is for us to
rebuild our lives with hands still
trembling. i know this with all that
is in me. these human hearts are
stronger than we think.

ullie-kaye

the path.

if you are in need of light, go to
the ones who have been through the
darkness. they will guide you. if you
are in need of hope, go to the ones
who have lost everything and somehow
still sing hallelujah. they will show
you the way. if you are in need of
strength, go to the ones who have been
down on their knees, feeble and broken
and weak to the bone. they will know how
to gather up the courage to get back up
on fractured limbs and walk or run or
begin their freedom march. if you need
love, go to the ones who have been without.
who longed but were forgotten. who sought
but were neglected. who dreamed but were
not given a chance. they will understand
the depths to which love can save a soul.
sometimes the path to knowledge is simply
in a human whose shoes are worn but whose
heart is willing. look for the one with
dust on his sandals and a cross on his
shoulders. he knows the way.

ullie-kaye

53

try again.

guard your heart, precious one.
do not let yourself grow cold.
stay soft even when the earth
around you rumbles and roars.
if you cannot move mountains,
move a stone. listen to the stories
of those who have lost everything-
they know the secret to overcoming.
know your worth and do not settle.
settling is for morning dew or
dust after the winds blow through.
carry your crosses. search for light.
make art out of whatever beauty
you manage to extract from the pain.
leave some room for mistakes.
show yourself grace. find the way.
then try again. always try again.

ullie-kaye

lost.

one of the greatest tragedies
of life is being so afraid of the
unknown that we find ourselves
at a crossroads. the water's edge.
the foot of a mountain. so lost
and unsure of where it might lead
that we could be standing at the
start of something so beautiful
and never even know it. how human
of us to lose so much because we
would rather stay where we already
recognize the soil.

ullie-kaye

yours.

i never wanted perfect love.
i wanted yours.
whatever floods.
whatever drought.
whatever windstorm.
whatever sunless, dreary days.
chosen. bloodied. broken. bruised.
i wanted yours.

　　　ullie-kaye

this too shall pass.

when people say, "this too shall pass",
i want to ask, "but when?". and in my
weakest moments, i resent my small faith
next to them. i wonder what they see and
if it's wisdom that they bring. how do
they know that flowers grow from the
roots of suffering? and then it dawns -
just like the sun. they too, have been
someplace before. in fields of want or
tides of pain and miles away from shore.
and i find myself believing that perhaps
the wounds we bleed, do not require things
made of fire but just a mustard seed.

ullie-kaye

57

love-filled.

i would have caught the rain with my
bare hands for you. held back the tides.
taken the storm away from your eyes.
i would have settled your sighs and kept
you warm. i would have brought you water
from the deepest well. saved you from
your earthly hell. and built the perfect
place for your heart to make a home.
but i knew you needed to fall a little.
fumble a little. grow a little. find your
way through. so i stood nearby instead,
just watching over you. and it was the
hardest, love-filled thing, that i have
ever had to do.

ullie-kaye

i miss you.

i miss you. and i cannot seem to undo the
emptiness that takes up all the space of
where you once so richly existed. of where
you once laughed your voice into my ribcage
and made me feel like i could do anything
that i set my mind and heart to. i miss the
way you held my broken pieces. and my bruises.
and told me it would be okay. and that even
if it wasn't, you'd be there. and that life was
made for doing together. i miss the way you
made the world seem just a little bit softer.
like i would land with feathers if i fell.
like the room would light up into a billion,
new colors or a billion, new stars. i miss how
i tried harder. because i dreamed bigger.
and how i dreamed bigger because i loved
better. and how i loved better because that's
how i was loved - by you. i was strong because
you taught me to use my weaknesses for good.
to give even when i was tired. and to follow
the light. always follow the light. to trust
the father, the son and the holy ghost.
that's what i miss the most.

ullie-kaye

59

make peace.

and if i may ask you
one thing, make peace
with it. whatever it is
that wakes you from
your sleep. whatever
it is that breaks you
into portions. whatever
it is that hunts you
like a thief and robs
you in broad daylight.
make peace. make peace.
make peace.

ullie-kaye

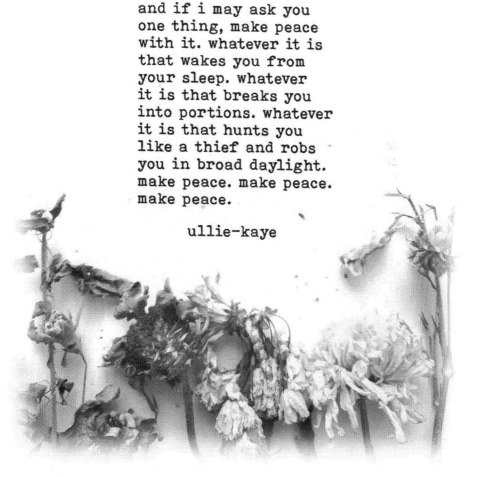

through.

you can grow up in chaos and become
someone who creates peace. you can grow
up being hurt and become someone who
looks tenderly after the wounds of others.
you can grow up being taught to turn
bitter from all of the wretched things
they did to you and become someone who
learns to forgive and move onward and
upward and forward. you can grow up
around anger and become a gentle spirit.
you can grow up surrounded by artificial
love and come to know how to recognize
real love. your history does not determine
whether or not you have the ability to
become a decent human being. in fact,
it can spur you on to break the cycle.
you have become who you are today because
you chose the future over your past.
because you dug through rather than
walked around. and because you needed to
be the very thing that was absent in
your life.

ullie-kaye

61

it was you.

i came to you with my wounds and
you saw my worthiness. i came to
you with my broken and brittle
and you saw my beautiful. i came
to you with walls so high, i thought
no one would ever dare to climb them.
you told me you only saw mountains
that had yet to be moved – and so
you moved them. i felt alone.
you invited me in. it was cold and
you held out your hands like a fire.
and i began to understand that there
was nowhere i could go, nowhere i
could run to where your presence
would not be made known. you were
in my deep waters. my unknown places.
my breathless void. it was you.
all along, it was you.

ullie-kaye

baby steps.

they may not always notice
the small changes that you
are making. make them anyway.
i swear this to be true. our
desire to get better needs to
stay greater than the fear that
keeps us from moving forward.
that is how we eventually get
there. by a thousand, painful,
baby steps. not by leaps and
bounds.

ullie-kaye

carried.

what does not kill you will not always
make you stronger. but that's okay.
we are not called to be strong. we are
called to persevere while we are yet weak.
to hold on with brittle hands. to inhale
when breath feels scarce. to grow our
roots from blackest soil. to believe in
the kind of love that does not only hold
you when you are full of sunlight, it
holds you, starless. heavy. empty. and cold.
what does not kill you will not always
make you stronger - i know this for certain.
but it will ask you this. to trust that in
your darkest hour, you are being carried.

ullie-kaye

the other side.

i am almost certain that i have yet
to meet people who will love me beyond
comprehension. and i am almost certain,
that i will love them tremendously too.
but i am also certain that there will
be people who will go. one way or another,
they will fall out of my life or walk on
through to the beauty that waits on the
other side. and what troubles me the most,
is that there will be people who leave -
when i am not even close to done with
loving them yet.

ullie-kaye

sometimes my heart.

sometimes my heart uses its running
feet instead of its walking feet.
it does not wait for a green light.
it barrels through like a storm without
a quiet place to land upon. it does
not find rest but rather thinks of
every possibility that does not come
with a happy ending. sometimes my heart
hurts like a steady ache that will not
go away. it holds in all of the things
that should be released. set free.
sent skyward. it does not listen to the
part of me that is begging for slow
breaths and deep thought and intentional
silences. sometimes my heart believes
it is an anchor. and so it tries to weigh
itself down, thinking it is staying put
when it is really staying empty of
ambition. it does not want to leave
familiar waters and would rather be
chained and aimless than untethered
and in unknown territory. sometimes my
heart loves more than it wants to and
breaks easier than it should. but then
sometimes i remember what a mighty
thing it is - to have a heart at all.

ullie-kaye

dear soul.

i can't do this on my own anymore.
- you don't have to.
i am complicated and layered and messy.
- i will meet you exactly where you are.
  take my hand.
but if you only knew about my past..
- i already do and that's where it will
  stay.
my bones are too battered and broken
to heal.
- your broken bones are my broken bones.
  let me in.
but i have too much for you to hold.
- dear soul, i have never met a burden
  that i could not carry.

ullie-kaye

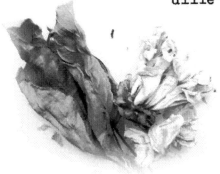

beside me.

if you want to understand me fully,
meet me in the storm. if you want to
help me forward, do not push me or
convince me or tell me that it is not
as big as it appears. tell me that i will
feel as though i have been ripped apart
by an army. by a sea of rising tides.
by mountains and beasts and unfriendly
skies. tell me that you see how its hands
are curled around my throat.
how it drenches me in ways that are not
refreshing for the soul. that you can
almost taste the way the wind has made
me wild for healing. that you see me trying.
and that i will somehow gather up the
strength to look up and ride it through.
that hope still lives inside my eyes.
that it's okay for me to cry. tell me that.
then walk beside me.

                    ullie-kaye

here you are.

what if i never heal?
- what would you call healing?
i mean, what if my life stays like this
forever?
- forever is certainly a long time.
i don't feel strong. not anymore.
- but do you feel grown?
what do you mean?
- have you become...
become what?
- closer to the person that resembles
  the soul that lives inside of you.
sometimes i look at myself and i wonder
how i ever made it this far.
- and yet here you are.
and sometimes i see how different i am
from how i was before.
how so?
i do not wait for life to come to me.
i live in the moment. i cling solely
to one fraction of peace at a time.
i am grateful for the smallest things.
the grace. the reprieve. the breaths
in between.
- then, my love, look closely.
  you have already healed.

ullie-kaye

falling together.

why do you love me this way?
   which way?
broken.
   why would i not?
because it can't be easy.
   i never asked for easy.
   i hung on a cross, remember?
but i am so complex.
   yes you are. it's how i made you.
   intricate.
how do you keep seeing the good in me
even after all this time?
   because i chose you.
chose me - for what?
   to be loved. not as the world loves
   but beyond reason and boundaries
   and comprehension.
and what do you want from me?
   trust.
it's hard to trust when everything keeps
falling apart.
   i know. believe me, i know.
   but sometimes your falling apart
   is really a falling together.

        ullie-kaye

70

scars.

i hope my scars never fade
completely. that way people
who see them will always
know that they have someone
they can talk to. my pain
does not need to define me
but it will refine me.
and there is no better story
to tell than that of a life
changed by the very fire that
tried to take you.

ullie-kaye

shelter.

whenever the storm comes. whenever
it shakes me up and turns me inside
out. when i am scattered at the mere
thought of going through this yet
again. and wonder how my fragile
bones shall even tolerate the winds.
the war. the wilderness. and what if
i can't. or what if i fail. and what
if i fall. i seek asylum in the silence.
i remember that there is shelter in
the midst of it all. there are deep
breaths. and angels. and people who
love me. and that fear is just peace
interrupted.

ullie-kaye

better place.

tomorrow will be better, right?
- that depends. what do you mean
  by better?
anything better than today.
- tell me about today so that i can
  help you with tomorrow.
i just felt so deeply hopeless and so
terribly lost and the kind of tired
that does not go away with sleep.
- oh, you mean you felt defeated.
yes, everywhere i looked, i only saw
the ruins of what once was and every
direction i tried to run, i was met
with another obstacle.
- you never ran.
what do you mean? i have run for most
of my life. everywhere i go, i leave a
wake of broken pieces.
- you never ran - to ME. you don't need
  a better tomorrow, my child, you need
  a better place to run to.

ullie-kaye

the rain.

i love the rain the most when it falls.
it reminds me so deeply of letting go.
of releasing everything that i have
absorbed over the years. carried in my
heart just a little too long. all those
things that have accumulated in the
clouds of my soul. taking up space.
welling up. and weighing me down.
waiting for the perfect, "i can do this"
moment. only to learn that there is
never really a wrong time when it comes
to freeing myself from the burdens.
even if i must be drenched in overcoming.
just look at the grasses after a storm.
they know. i love the rain the most
when it falls.

ullie-kaye

mountains.

some of us have big emotions and nowhere
to release them. some of us are carrying
more than our fair share of burdens but still
hanging on by whatever means we possibly
can. some of us have a story so profound
but feel too numb to splatter it across ocean
waves. so instead it sits crumpled up in a
bottle, flowing with the tides, just waiting for
someone to happen upon it. some of us are
deeply wounded and do not know how to
breathe without collapsed lungs and broken
spirits. some of us are still learning to trust
because everything we have experienced
in life, has given us another reason not to.
some of us only know how to give until we are
trampled upon by those who take advantage
of kind hearts and have yet to know how to
say no. some of us feel trapped in a past
that we cannot erase and don't know how
to move beyond how deep the chasm of our
trauma is. and so we climb these hills.
we carry our crosses. and if we are fortunate
enough, we have those who wander beside us.
satchels on. sometimes marching. sometimes
falling. but always gathering ourselves back
up again. whether fear or pain or love and loss.
the truth is, we all have our mountains.

ullie-kaye

75

wildly.

may we live each day in such a way
that fear itself is afraid to haunt us.
may we run wildly but always towards
those slivers and cracks of light that
illuminate the darkness. may we cheer
each other on because goodness knows
how much we all need it. may we never
sink so low that we do not recognize
our own spirit. may we choose wisdom
and tenderness over careless words.
heartfelt emotion over empty gestures.
quiet giving over loud acts of charity.
may we rather forgive too often than
not enough. may we always strive to
see beauty. even if we must squint our
eyes and tilt our heads to find it.

ullie-kaye

sometimes grief.

where does love go when the other
is gone. where is the light that once
brightly shone. does it wait at the
border of here and of there.
does it lift up on wings. does it rise
in a prayer. is love that still lives
just a breath from uniting. is it always
a flame, does the fire keep igniting.
where does love go. does it sit on
a bench. is it written on stone. is it
thirsty or quenched. is love that once
sounded like sunshine, alive when the
clouds roll on in and the storms move
inside. sometimes grief is the shape
of a heart's empty spaces. but love
finds a way for the things time erases.

ullie-kaye

introvert.

i am an introvert through and through.
i bury my heart in the quieter places.
i look for ways to busy myself doing the
things that no one sees but matter deeply
to me. i am absolutely content walking
alone. being one with nature. tending to
my garden of thoughts. wondering how
i will ever sort them. or change them.
or tame them from their wilderness.
i am overly aware of everything.
i am constantly imagining the feelings
of others. what mighty things they have
endured. or what mountains they have had
to climb. whether they dream in color or
in black and white. and where does their
mind go when their eyes trail off into
the distance like that. i see one cloud
and i envision a storm, raging. rumbling.
tumbling. releasing its strength towards
those who just needed a moment of refreshing.
i see one brave soul and i envision an army.
i see the twinkling of one light and i
envision a sky filled to the brim with stars
so beautiful, they make me want to be a
better person. and so i try. i always try.

ullie-kaye

love letter.

dear you. yes you. are you tired too?
i have been walking this path with you
for as long as i can remember and i was
wondering why we have never met before.
although i did recognize the heaviness in
your footsteps from a mile away.
i recognized the way you drew your breath
as though your lungs were perforated.
and i recognized that big heart of yours
that is sometimes too big for your own good.
i saw you stumble a little and murmur
something quietly and i just wanted to make
sure that you were okay. are you? i mean really
okay. if you don't mind, i would love to give
you something. don't feel obligated at all.
but i made you this. see this box? it's handcarved.
open it. oh. i know it's empty, that's because
you haven't let me fill it yet. there's so much
goodness for you to gather. but you never
let yourself believe that those things were
meant for you. they were all for you.
they were all – for you. and oh and by the way,
i heard what you said in the tunnel. come.
the light is this way.

ullie-kaye

an easy life.

i don't understand.
- well you have come to the right place.
i don't understand pain. or suffering.
or why some people have an easy life
and seem to coast along without a care
in the world.
- do you want an easy life?
i mean, i wouldn't mind having some
reprieve once in awhile.
- i asked if you wanted an easy life.
well, not completely easy, no.
- so you want me to orchestrate just enough
easy to keep you happy but just enough hard
to keep you growing, is that it?
when you put it that way it does sound
rather shallow.
- my child. have you forgotten already?
that i'm strong?
- no. that I AM.

ullie-kaye

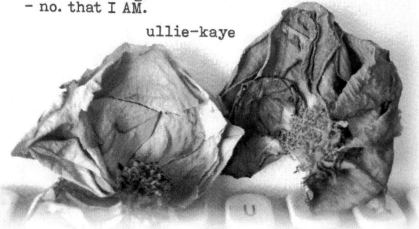

anchor.

don't you understand?
your heart needed to break
in order to become an anchor.
it needed to plunge, heavy.
it needed to sink and struggle
and dig its roots down hard
into the ocean floor.
and it needed reckless and
uncertain waters before it
knew it had a place to land.

ullie-kaye

burning.

i carved a sun today.
out of every broken part of me that said
i was made up of too much rain. i tried
glowing and was surprised to see how
beautiful the light can be. how sometimes
the storm can share the same sky with
the dawn. and sing the same song.
and how bravely their souls get along.
i breathed out fire today.
i let it simmer down into my deepest pores.
i let it ruin me in whatever places i needed
refreshing the most. and then i grew an
orchard from all of the remnants. brand new.
with trees through and through. lush.
and vibrant. and rich with dew.
i made love my anthem.
i played it loud every morning to awaken
my spirit and every night to make peace
out of all the restlessness in me. miles and
miles of unlearning. i played it for every
heart that would listen and every heart that
had never even heard the sound. and i trembled
a little at the thought of how good it felt –
to be burning.

ullie-kaye

rest.

it takes enormous strength to carry
our burdens. but we cannot underestimate
the strength it takes to admit when they
have become too heavy. surrender is not
weakness. it is knowing when enough is
enough. it is feeling and honoring what
you have and have not been called to bear.
show yourself the same grace that in a
fraction of a heartbeat, you would extend
to someone else. the last thing we need
is a world full of people who are barely
hanging on. find some shelter and stay
for as long as your soul requires it.
this journey was not meant to be taken
without setting your bags down and stopping
to rest for awhile.

ullie-kaye

my heart.

my heart is a little bit bent. it is a
little bit crumpled, misshapen, worn out
and tired. sometimes it is too full of
emotions and too empty of sensible
thought. and if i may, there are a few
blemishes from having been trampled.
walked on. thrown to the side. there are
still remnants of makeshift ways i tried
to stitch it back together. needle and
thread, band-aids and glue that never
seemed to hold. it is still tender to the
touch from believing the wrong things
and taking the wrong turns and trusting
the wrong people. sometimes it startles
even at the sound of something good.
it beats too fast. it runs away instead of
towards. it hides itself in anything that
will lessen the pain for the moment.
but oh has it ever loved - deep into the
ends of the earth. even with the edges
worn and its chambers brittle. it is all
that i can give you.

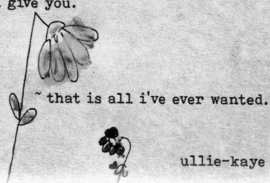

~ that is all i've ever wanted.

ullie-kaye

run.

you will need to stop running
in order to feel the silence.
and you will need to feel the
silence in order to face the
fear. and you will need to face
the fear in order to undo its
grip. and you will need to undo
its grip in order to run. but
darling, run freely, not away.

ullie-kaye

phases.

i was lost.
  and i loved you.
i was far from who you wanted me to be.
  and i loved you.
i was unforgiving and stubborn and
did things my own way.
  and i loved you.
i shut you out. i walked away. i turned
my back on you.
  you're here now, aren't you?
i have nowhere left to go –
why do you keep staying?
  because my love reaches far. it yearns
  for you. it follows you to the depths
  of every dark place and every wretched
  storm. it is i who whispered in your ear.
what did you say?
  i will love you in all of your phases.

            ullie-kaye

sadness and beauty.

why do sadness and beauty evoke
the same emotion? because there is
something within beauty that stirs
us to tears. and there is something
within sadness that reminds us
of beauty. it is all intertwined,
don't you see? the things that take
our breath away, also fill us with
wonder. and wonder, whether it is in
awe or despair, keeps us ever searching
for the deeper meaning of things.

ullie-kaye

messy.

here's my heart. it's messy.
- that's okay.
it's bruised.
- that's okay.
it's tender.
- that's okay.
it wanders off the path sometimes.
- that's okay. do you have room?
room for what?
- love.
it's all i want.
- then come, i have places to show you.

ullie-kaye

"not yet".

i almost said, "i can't" today.
it sat on the tip of my tongue.
it lingered in every breath that
i took and it roared inside of my
lungs. i felt my bones weaken,
i felt my mind churn and every
right thing turned to wrong.
i stifled my praise as i counted
the ways i had once again failed
to be strong. but a faint voice
inside me, a spirit of truth,
began stirring like winds made
of thunder. it urged me to sit in
the still of my heart and rephrase
the words pulling me under.
so instead of "i can't", i whispered –
"not yet", my voice was trembling
but sure. and perhaps "i'm not able"
is merely a fable of things i've
been asked to endure.

ullie-kaye

fixed.

we weren't the kind
of broken that needed
to be fixed.
we just needed to be
listened to.

ullie-kaye

bright.

before you go, i want you
to know; i cannot love the
darkness out of you. but i
will wave this light for as
long as it takes. until my
arms grow tired and even then.
i will rub my bones to make
fire. i will stay bright for
you.
                ullie-kaye

"see you later".

i have learned a few things about grief.
it is not a temporary feeling but rather
an eternal one with many changing seasons.
grief hurts in places that are hard to point
to because the pain in your heart overflows
into every other crevice that exists inside
of your body. sometimes grief longs to be
held and pushes you away at the same time.
it runs for both freedom and shelter.
it wants to heal but without letting go.
grief lands upon your chest whenever and
however and wherever it chooses. it is not
bound by space or time or distance and i can
guarantee you that it will always find a way
to come to the surface. grief lays its weary
head down and waits for rain. for sun.
for wild winds. for peace - oh precious,
precious peace. grief reminds us that death
is not a goodbye. but the longest and hardest
"see you later"..

ullie-kaye

piece of fire.

i do not ask for much. just let me live
the way that i know best. let me feel
the earth on my feet and rejoice that
i am still standing. let me listen to the
waves of the sea and find peace in
knowing that the tides always return
to wash over me. let me dream about
sunsets that are not promised and skies
that are not always blue. let me make
love to conversations that bring me
closer to knowing myself and closer to
believing in something much bigger than
the four, square walls of my own chest.
and let me rest. oh lord, let me rest.
and should i be so blessed to have this
place where i can grow, let me remember
to give more than i receive. to listen more
than i speak. and to understand that
everyone is searching for a little piece
of fire. may i take part in building that.

ullie-kaye

93

fly away.

did you feel that - the flutter in your
chest that we call breath? it was a fresh
start. there it is again, a new beginning.
do not believe for even a moment that you
have lost your purpose here. you have just
been through some wild waters. your world
has just collapsed into a thousand, unheard
pieces. everything weighs heavy. and hurts.
and feels so deep and dark and uncertain.
you have quietly wished to fly away.
to find someplace else for your heart to land.
to fall asleep and wake up healed. ungrieved.
or unlonely. listen, brave soul. you are here
because your life is still so full of gold
and grace and holding on. and as hard as
it gets, be still and know. the earth is more
beautiful with you inside of it.

ullie-kaye

as i found you.

they cannot tell me how to grieve.
these mourning hands already know.
i pick the flowers without petals; those
brittle-stemmed blooms that have lost
some of their shimmer. i set them on the
table and i admire their beauty even in
the absence of exuberance. how they still
try to stand tall. and brave. and make the
room a little brighter for me. i look up
at heaven and notice the lonesome cloud,
drifting softly away from the others,
finding its own piece of land to call home.
somewhere between the vast expanse of
glowing stars and the falling ones.
they cannot tell me how to grieve.
these mourning hands already know.
i watch the sky and wonder how the rain
chooses whom to drown and whom to bring
refreshing. does it even care that i am here
and you are there, or is it weeping too?
sending condolences in storm shaped
envelopes to open or scatter or cherish or
lay beside my pillow forever.
or maybe just for now.
for now, i shall love you as i found you.
as though you were still here, eating pumpkin
pie and laughing your smile into every ounce
of my bloodstream. it is how you would
want me to be. living - but a little more
tenderly.

ullie-kaye

95

human.

i don't need much. i prefer to live simply
and quietly. anything that takes away
from my authentic self, is not worth my
time or energy. i am sincere. and curious.
and ask way too many questions – but only
because i am constantly trying to figure
out where i belong and how i can do better.
i hurt easily but forgive just as easily.
i have known brokenness and therefore often
tread with caution. i long for wisdom and
search for it more urgently with every
passing day. but i long too, for things
of the heart. like peace. and compassion.
and small acts of bravery. i am steadfast
in hope but still lose my way. i am human.

ullie-kaye

holes.

i wonder if those who have the biggest
holes in their hearts are also the ones
who have the greatest capacity to let
the light come in. to love. and give.
and weep their sorrows into gratitude.
that is to say, sometimes brokenness
has a way of cracking you right down
to your barest parts. and when you have
nothing left to hide, nowhere left to go
and no one left beside you, you can either
choose to become a boarded up wall or a
wide open window.

ullie-kaye

the things we do.

when we lose someone that we once loved,
oceans do not merely toss and tumble before
our eyes. they land upon our skin and drench
our souls with memories of another time.
their tides consume the parts of us that
loved so hard and so softly. so fiercely and
so deeply. they do not just sound like waves,
scurrying about but rather the rushing of
a rhythmic heartbeat that we used to know.
when we lose someone that we once loved,
the trees do not merely sway their branches
to and fro. they whisper. and bow. and make
an archway for us to gather up the fallen
leaves. the fallen branches. the fallen seeds
that will no longer grow. and we see the art.
the artist. how beautifully the life that once
was - is still living. still breathing.
still singing their songs into our lungs.
when we lose someone that we once loved,
the chesterfield becomes an orchard. we wander
'round the flowerbeds, the blossoms and hills
and find where the skies meet the sea. and we
stay for awhile. we do not hurry the moment.
we notice how the clouds look like the perfect
shape of the space where they once so richly
existed. because love does not go away. it does
not take a boat and land upon a distant shore.
it lingers. it longs. it waits for the greatest
reunion of all. these are the things we do.

ullie-kaye

98

always and forever.

i just don't think i have the
strength anymore.
so i was wondering if i could
borrow some of yours.

you need not borrow my strength.
keep it. always and forever.
inside your heart.
tucked under your ribcage.
in the storm.
the tunnel.
the unrelenting tides.
my strength is your strength.
i'd hang the stars for you.

ullie-kaye

so you think i'm strong.

so you think i'm strong? then you
have never met me in the darkness;
my hands folded together in grief.
my eyes; rivers that can not stop
flowing. bones that have dried up
into deserts. you have never met me
where fear seizes my breath. where
i am too numb to move and too tired
to try. you think i'm strong? then
you have never met me in the silence;
my body aching to make sense of it all.
my mind wandering wild to places that
it should not go. places that do not
heal me or grow me or lift up my spirit.
where quiet hurts because quiet lets
me think. and thinking hurts because
thinking makes me remember. and where
remembering just makes me hurt all
over again. you think i'm strong?
then you have never met me in all of
the storms where i ran for shelter and
in all of the races that i had to quit.
you haven't seen me fall apart at the
seams. drunk on defeat. rock bottom
low. nowhere to go - but to Him.

ullie-kaye

especially then.

please don't go. not yet.
there is still so much i have planned
for you. so many places to show you.
so many things to teach you about
growing and grieving and flying and
falling. and so many more ways to say,
"i love you" even when you are on the
darkest stretches of the road.
the wooded groves. the starless nights.
the fire scattered to the wind.
- especially then.

ullie-kaye

dwelling place.

there are things that they can never
take away from you. deep soul kind
of things. this is where your wonder
blossoms. there in those quiet chambers
where the light you've tended to so
diligently over the passage of time,
still glows. the ever burning fire that
cannot be extinguished. this is your
dwelling place. your temple. your years
of growth merged with the inner silences
of peace. you hold the key and grant
the access, no one else. but should they
come one day and try to change who you
are. to question your beauty. to instill
doubt upon your path, remember who
lives there. and do not give anyone that
kind of power over you.

ullie-kaye

as you are.

the ones who love you as you are. who see
your dark and do not run but rather have
this way of gently leading you towards the
light. the ones who recognize that sometimes
you will distance yourself when you probably
need them the most and so they find new
ways to stay close. and check in. and leave
their remnants of compassion at your doorstep
instead. the ones who understand that your
laughter does not always match what you are
feeling on the inside. and that sometimes when
it seems like you are not trying, you are just
forging another path. the ones who are
prepared to see you at your worst and sit
with you in silence. in those uncomfortable
places that are too deep for words to reach.
the ones who advocate for you behind closed
doors. who fight. and pray. and do the heavy
work without being asked. who remember how
you used to dance in the rain and are willing
to make a fool of themselves in the name of
bringing you back to life for one, glorious
fraction of time. and so you dance. and raise
your hands. and drench yourself in the moment.
in the magic. in the mystery of freedom.
and faith. and fullness. the ones who are not
afraid of the storm. but know there is a time
for shelter too. these are my kind of people.

ullie-kaye

103

this or that.

i suppose one of the most beautiful and
terrifying things that i have ever come
to know is how vastly different our hearts
can be. some are cities with ruins piled
high, bracing for the aftershocks that still
wake and shake their souls to the core
every morning. some are twinkling lights,
just trying to be seen for a single breath
of time. "look. here i am, still shining.
i'm living. i'm dying. i'm somewhere in
between. remember me?". some are ominous
skies about to give way to a storm or perhaps
always just on the verge, uncertain of
whether to hold on or let go. but it feels
uneasy. and heavy. and so very uncomfortable.
some are trees that burst with color for a
season and then grow cold and empty and bare.
stretching their limbs as far and wide as
they can but at the constant mercy of the
next wild wind that topples them over.
and then there are the mountains, those
fierce and protective giants of the earth.
believing they must always be strong and
untouchable yet inside they are yearning
to be a pebble for just one day. to crumble.
and fall. to soften. to break. to sway like
the branches. to weep like the skies. to twinkle
like starlight with ruins piled high.
this is why we mustn't go about assuming one
is this or that. there are layers upon layers
everywhere.

ullie-kaye

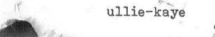

the bright side.

and for the record, you do not
need to pretend that you have
it all together. it is perfectly
acceptable to fall apart.
to be overcome by emotion.
to yearn and ache and bleed for
better days. to wake up feeling
heavy. and brittle. and full of
the kind of darkness that seems
impossible to shake. and if you
ever feel as though you must keep
only the bright side of the moon
visible, then my love, perhaps
you are surrounding yourself
with the wrong kind of people.

ullie-kaye

so free.

i want to be so free that my lungs speak
to each other in fresh breezes and soft
words, whispered in a language that only
i and the angels fully understand.
i want my arms to believe in flying again.
to skydive in and out of every treetop that
i have only ever seen from the roots up.
grounded in hope but airborne in redemption.
i want to hold on to nothing at all but sweet
mercy and the mighty mover of mountains;
carrying echoes from those souls who are
already long gone from earth but whose
fire will always burn bright from within
my spirit. i want to roar like a lion who
knows that this is only the beginning.
that love is alive and well and winning.
and that every broken part of me is art.
and a message. and a gift. and a planted seed.
that's how free i want to be.

ullie-kaye

of missing.

time is strange. sometimes i cannot bend
my mind around how quickly it disappears
into thin air. turns the corner and floats
away. never to be seen or heard from again –
except in those whispers that linger and
long. the ones that remind me that i am still
here and you are there. and then it slows
right down to moving in fractions of seconds
again. watching dewdrops melt on blades of
grass. and counting how many trees have
yet to empty themselves of their leaves.
on my street. this autumn. or next. or even
the season after that. and wondering when
i will ever see the arms that have literally
held me together piece by piece through all
of this. until then, i will be a soul,
wrapped in a body, waiting to be a soul,
wrapped in starlight. i will string together
breaths from every hour of every painstaking
day and i will make something beautiful
of missing. somehow i feel you closest then.

ullie-kaye

unloved.

do you know what happens when
you grow up feeling unloved?
you either make sure it stays that
way. you build your walls high and
live wherever love is scarce.
or you settle for any version of love
that comes along even if it isn't love
at all. because it is the only thing
your heart has ever recognized.
or you spend the rest of your life
on earth, making sure that no one
else who crosses your path, will ever
have to feel that way.

ullie-kaye

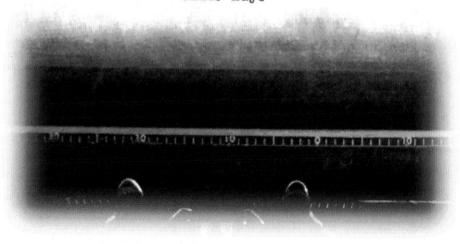

someplace kind.

take me someplace kind.
where sunsets can be watched in slow
motion. and every part of the sky at
every, single moment of its surrender
to nightfall, is kept like sequenced
photographs. on my wall of 'things that
bring me peace'. take me someplace kind.
where the syrup on my pancakes stops
disappearing. and i remember that i don't
always have to see love to know that it is
sweet. and it doesn't always have to be
sweet to be good. and that good love is
the best love. even if it isn't perfect.
take me someplace kind. where the air
sings lullabies and i am a five year old all
over again with wonder inside of my eyes.
and i haven't yet learned what it means to
grieve. or hurt. or hide – who i am.
because i still believe that everyone is
beautiful. everyone IS beautiful, aren't they?
or has that changed? take me someplace
kind. where shallow is the part of the pool
that i am allowed to swim in. not a way
of being. where tenderness does not mean
weakness. and strength does not mean
holding it in. where hope is a billboard so
wide and so tall, it needs no introduction
at all. because everybody knows it.
everybody knows it. take me someplace kind.

ullie-kaye

tremble and heal.

come cry with me. you will feel a little lighter,
i promise you. let us release these storms back
into the wind where they can turn into stories
of who we became from endurung it all.
let us carry one another's oceans and watch
as the tides try to take us but retreat at the
strength that comes where two or three are
gathered. come cry with me. we can splatter
our souls into the sky and be starlight together;
drinking every last drop of the wild wonder that
we have named life. where our broken pieces
will fit perfectly into someone else's emptiness.
where love reaches around every one of these
hurts and lands itself upon our sadness with so
much grace that it changes absolutely everything.
and may we never be the same. we will tremble
through this. tremble and heal. tremble and heal.

ullie-kaye

ready.

why do we spend so much of our time on healing?
- i suppose it's because you have been through
  a great deal of hurting.
but do we ever arrive?
- that depends on your destination.
i don't always know which way i'm going
or if i'm getting any closer.
- you will know when you are arriving.
how?
- because you will be ready to climb mountains
  and cross oceans and walk straight into the
  storm for it.
i guess it's the best gift i can give myself then.
- oh, my love, it is much more than that.
  your healing is the best gift to everyone
  that crosses your path.

ullie-kaye

new normal.

i don't think we talk enough about
how quiet the road gets. how long
the waiting feels. how lonely healing
can be. i don't think we talk enough
about how undone we become in the
valley of grief. or how enormously we
must stretch just to fit ourselves into
some kind of a new normal and dare
to call it life again. and i don't think
we talk enough about how we have no
other thing left but to gather up our
heavy limbs and carry on. because the
earth keeps on spinning. the sun keeps
on rising. and the days keep on bleeding,
one into the next, regardless of the
moment that made all the minutes inside
of our heart stand still.

ullie-kaye

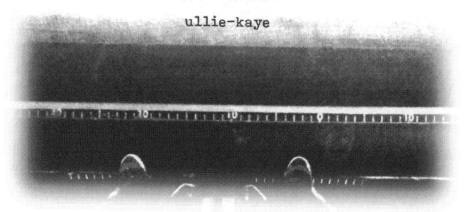

next door.

and when you miss me most, remember
that i have only built a house next door.
a single breath away. we can whisper
through the walls and send love notes
in the shape of stars and sunsets and
the way that the light glistens on the
water just so. and although things are
hard for you now, i am not far away.
i am absent only in flesh but my spirit
is dancing with the heavenly ones. we will
reach each other once again - i promise.
just not yet. find laughter again, okay?
find music and purpose and ways to feel
alive. we are only separated by a glimmer
of time. an interval. take comfort.
i have only built a house next door.

ullie-kaye

for awhile.

and for awhile it will feel as though
you have all of this love but nowhere
to bring it. and if you do, give it to
the smallest of creatures. however you
find them. breadcrumbs for the birds.
a tender hand for the butterfly with
the crooked wings. cup your hands and
save the insects from drowning.
give your love to the wandering ones.
those souls who do not quite know how
to find their way in an unforgiving world.
give your love to the days where the sun
does not make an appearance. where oceans
are deep and unkind and relentless.
to the loneliest tree in the quietest orchard.
find me here. beside every act of courage.
amongst the beauty and the ache.
scratched into backs of park benches and
beach sands and pavement on rainy days.
i am woven into every memory that we've
ever made. when your love has nowhere to go,
give it away. and wherever it lands,
that's where i am too.

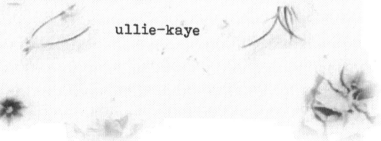

ullie-kaye

how to live.

what i would not give to have you sit
with me for one more hour. i have so
much to tell you and and so much more
to give you. i broke in two the day you
left this earth to live in that mansion
just over the hilltop. i never knew how
much one, single moment could fracture
absolutely every bone in my body.
but i will be okay. perhaps not yet but
i am working on it every day. and i want
you to know that i have grown into someone
who has learned how to keep on going
when the world collapses all around me.
i am gentler now. and braver. i do not take
this breath for granted. i still miss you
every day – that will never change.
but i think that you would love who i have
become and the way that i have chosen
to honor you. to keep your beautiful heart
present in everything i do. i am a better
person not only because of who you were
but because i lost someone who showed me
how to live.

ullie-kaye

flying.

are we not all like
these injured birds?
flightless and weak
and tired of trying.
and yet somewhere within,
whether winged or with skin,
we know we were made for
flying.

ullie-kaye

nothing at all.

i want you to know that i will
never try to take your grief
and make it into something small.
neither will i tell you that the
sun will come and shine again
and spill itself upon your wall.
i will not tell you that the better
place that they are in should
soften how you fall. nor bring
the mountains into view and say,
"see, they're not so tall".
i hope that on that dreary day
when your life comes to a crawl,
i search my heart, i hug you close
and say nothing at all.

ullie-kaye

moving on.

you see, a part of me will always
be missing. there are gaping holes
where you once shone your light so
bravely and richly into this world.
and it's not that i haven't grown and
healed more than i ever thought i
would. or could. or even wanted to.
but the truth is, i have kept these
pieces of your life so tenderly inside
of my heart, that sometimes i just
want to stay empty and broken for
a little while longer. perhaps it is
the letting go that i fear the most.
because letting go might mean forgetting.
and forgetting means fading away.
and fading away means moving on.
and some days i just don't feel ready
to fly the sky without you.

                ullie-kaye

nothing lasts forever.

nothing lasts forever. except for matters
of the heart. and the memories of all that
you have had to fight for. the things you
lived for and the things you would never
hesitate to die for. nothing lasts forever.
except for the imprint of souls that loved
you at your worst. souls that always saw
the best in you. and souls whose light burned
out on earth but went on to shine where
bodies become spirits and spirits are clothed
in everlasting garments. nothing lasts forever.
except for those words like flowers that
make their way into your mind and plant a
garden. or quiet a storm. or silence an ache.
words that piece you back together and
remind you that you were made in image of
holiness. a church with bells ringing. a sky
with stars singing. and every good gift that
the Maker is bringing. nothing lasts forever.
or so they say.

                    ullie-kaye

sunrise and sunset.

what is this thing that we call grief.
is it really love or is it a beast.
if it is love then why does it hurt.
and if it's a beast then why are these
feet not running away. for shelter.
for freedom. for a safe place to stay.
why is my heart both softened and
raging. and why does it feel like a
songbird some days with the wings of
a fire-breathing dragon. uncaging.
i am equally tender as i am full mourned.
a flowerbed of roses, half fragrant,
half thorned. and it's almost as though
i am watching the sky make sunrise
and sunset at the same time.
hello never hurts as much as goodbye.

ullie-kaye

the table.

keep your light shining.
there are some who are waiting for
the very thing you have tucked inside
of your soul. whether water for those
who thirst for belonging or earth for
those who cannot grow. whether music
for ears whose hope has been silenced
or a satchel for the ones who just cannot
carry it all. bring whatever you have
to the table. we will exchange our
parched lips for rain. or rugged soil
for tender gardens. our broken hearts
for the sound of healing. and the weight
of our burdens for perfect release.
come all. with your lanterns. your beacons.
your fireworks. and stars.
you're invited.

ullie-kaye

grief is just love.

we go about our lives, carrying a satchel.
and on the good days, we gather up all of
those beautiful and shiny things that catch
our attention. we stand in awe of nature
and our satchel glows and grows with sunsets
and stars and acts of kindness sent our way.
it overflows with memories that make us smile
and dreams we longed for that were never
promised but so graciously granted anyways.
and somehow regardless of what goes in,
our satchel is light and easy to strap on.
when grief comes along, it takes up so much
space. and we don't always quite know what
to do with it because it suddenly displaces all
of the good things we had so neatly folded in.
kept safely in compartments with zippers and
strings. and grief does not know where it fits
or where to go or how to be light. and so we
walk under the weight and spill some of the
dear contents to make room. and we wonder at
how emptiness can feel so terribly heavy.
yet we cannot deny how great an honor it is
to carry such a burden. and what we often fail
to recognize is that grief is just love with tears
on her face. either way, our satchel is full.

ullie-kaye

softened.

i want to plunge myself into beauty.
into art. and grace. and the human
condition. how we rise and how we fall,
sometimes within the same breath.
how some are prone to fear and wandering
while others seem to glide along like
birds in the open heavens; content to
stay in the moment, always finding their
way towards the light. i am mesmerized
by all of the things around me that
are crumbling. old buildings, stripped
to their bare bones, still standing tall
with dignity. poised against streams
of sun, hitting their windows just enough
to make a cathedral out of brokenness.
i too, long to be softened this way.

ullie-kaye

123

faith.

faith does not begin where fear ends.
she comes when you are still lying in
the bottom of the gutter. hands trembling.
doubts running rampant. seas stormy.
breath insufficient. darkness winning.
thoughts blurring. skies fading. more black
than blue. obstructed view. no way through.
there. in the absence. in the tragedy.
in the emptiness. in the wreckage that made
its way into the very marrow of your bones.
in the fire that could not be drenched.
in the thirst that could not be quenched.
in the wounds that would not heal. in the
heart that could not feel. in the broken.
the lost. and surreal. that's when she comes.

ullie-kaye

full circle.

full circle is holding the ones who
once held us. you will know when
this moment has arrived because
it will hit you like a ton of bricks.
like ocean waves. like petals falling.
slowly. softly. sacredly. out of season.
you will feel a sense of familiarity
and yet it will all feel so distant and
strange and new for your soul.
there is such a natural beauty about
caring for those who have devoted
their whole lives to our well-being.
whose light shone brighter when our
light shone brighter and whose light
faded a little when ours faded a little.
the hands of time teach us so much
about tenderness and love and trading
places. and sometimes even letting go.
this is full circle. where emptiness
collides with the wholeness of giving.

ullie-kaye

gold.

if they are still standing by
your side when your armor is off.
when your walls are down.
when your heart is broken.
and your scars are visible.
tuck them into your arms like gold
and do not let them go.

ullie-kaye

empath.

when you are an empath, ninety-eight
percent of the hurt in your heart is not
your own. two thirds of the seas inside
you are stormy. half of you wants to build
an ark and save as many as you can and
the other half is willing to go down in
the flood. when you are an empath, you
have one emotion and it remains nameless
because is there even a word for feeling
it all at once? when you are an empath,
you are both completely full and completely
empty. constantly hurting and constantly
healing. and i am almost one hundred
percent sure that it is both a blessing and
a curse. a gift and such a graceless way
to live. terribly beautiful and beautifully
terrifying. when you are an empath,
ninety-eight percent of the hurt in your
heart is not your own.

ullie-kaye

parachute and aeroplane.

i hope hope finds you.
i hope hope builds you a shelter when you
need a place to rest and scurries you out
when you become too comfortable in staying.
i hope hope never leaves you without a small
inkling of wonder, even in your most wretched
moments and perhaps even more so then.
i hope hope wraps around your shoulders like
a warm blanket. like a soft light. like a tender
reminder that your spirit has flown through
wild winds before and survived.
i hope hope never falls asleep and keeps the
door wide open. i hope hope does not make things
easier for you but rather more beautiful for
the soul that lives behind the walls that we
have named body. i hope hope finds you breathing,
receiving and believing in something and someone
much bigger and stretches your faith accordingly.
may hope be both your parachute and aeroplane.
my love, may you always fly and land where the
unknown air causes you to rely on more than
just your own two wings. because they will
always be insufficient. i hope hope finds you.

ullie-kaye

128

some days.

some days are hard. and when they are,
i allow myself to feel whatever it is
that my body asks me to feel and i respect
the time it needs to fumble and flounder
and fall a little. some days i am swallowed
whole by things too big for me to hold.
and so i set them down. i rest, knowing
that even when i cannot slay the beast,
i can lay aside my sword for a moment and
work on protecting my spirit instead.
some days my heart beats like thunder
inside of my chest. it is heavy. and loud.
and relentless. it does not listen to the
part of me that wants to silence the storm.
and so i take my eyes off of the noise and
fix them on quieter places. on music. and art.
and heaven. and trees. and i show myself
grace in the dark - even if i am shaking
my way through it. because some days i still
haven't caught my breath from yesterday yet.

ullie-kaye

129

beautiful things.

i keep seeing all of these beautiful
things and thinking how much you
would have loved them. and i keep
wanting to pick up the phone and
tell you everything.
but i am here and you are there.
and i can only imagine how you must
.be seeing the glistening lights of
heaven and thinking how much i'm
gonna love them too.

ullie-kaye

grow.

you don't need to get through
everything today. you don't
need to conquer the world.
slay the beasts. and raise your
sword in victory. and you never
need to apologize for taking time
to grow. sometimes healing is a
slow and quiet inner revolution.
let it come. beautiful things have
a way of falling into place.

ullie-kaye

to be continued.

life is so much bigger than we know.
death comes, yes but it is just a pause.
an intermission. to be continued...

ullie-kaye

love well now.

one day you will give them
your final hug. your final
"how are you?". your final
"i love you." and you may not
have the chance for them to
hear your final "goodbye."
love well now.

ullie-kaye

through you.

i tried to run away from grief.
it followed me.
i tried to bandage it up.
it split wide open.
i tried to push it down into my chest.
my heart began to burst.
i tried to hide it in a smile.
my tears still found a way.
i tried to bury it in the ground.
it sprouted and grew even bigger.
i kept myself busy.
it reached in and said,
"i'm not done with you yet."
grief cannot be walked around.
it must come through you.

ullie-kaye

empty spot.

why does it hurt?
 why does what hurt?
my heart.
 oh, that's the feeling of an empty spot.
will it ever go away?
 not completely.
what will happen?
 it will stay tender for a little awhile
 and sometimes for a longer while.
how do i fill it back up?
 you don't need to fill it with anything.
 keep it sacred.
how?
 remember the love that lived there once.
 it may not feel like it now but your empty
 spot is really ever so full.
it is?
 overflowing.
 your grief is a place holder for an entire
 ocean of love.
 it will always be a part of you.

ullie-kaye

enduring.

do not underestimate someone who
has lost everything and is still
here to tell the story. do not
underestimate someone who has
fought dearly for sobriety. peace.
forgiveness. self-love. freedom.
authenticity. truth. do not
underestimate the lonely. they
have braved wars that only those
who understand the absence of
human connection, can do.
even now, they are holding it all
together while coming so wildly
undone. and sometimes we may see
them unravel ever so softly. or
loudly. or however their soul
unties its cage the best. do not
underestimate the ones who have
suffered the kind of grief that
does not seem to end. who have been
broken in places you did not even
know existed. the ones who fell
into silence because their lungs
had no words left to speak. we will
not always be strong. no. but we
are enduring.

ullie-kaye

Made in the USA
Middletown, DE
12 August 2024

59024670R00077